All About Plants

by Leslie Ann Rotsky

PEARSON
Scott
Foresman

DK

What are the parts of a plant?

Plants need water, air, and sun.
Plants need space.
Plants need nutrients.
Nutrients are the food that living things need to grow.
Plants get nutrients from soil and water.

Plant Parts

Plants have four parts.
The parts are the roots, stem, leaves,
and flowers.
These parts help the plant get what it needs.

Roots grow into the soil.
Roots hold a plant in place.
Roots take water and nutrients from the soil to the stem.

The **stem** takes water and nutrients to the leaves.
The stem holds up the plant.

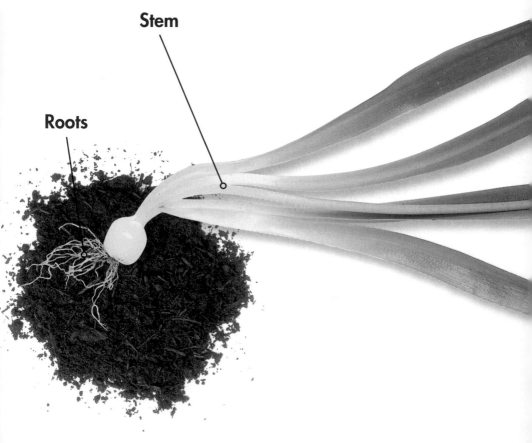

Stem

Roots

Leaves use sunlight, air, and water to make food for the plant.

Many plants have flowers. A **flower** makes seeds. Seeds make new plants.

Leaves

Flower

Seeds

How are seeds scattered?

Plants grow from seeds.
When seeds are spread out, they have
room to grow.
Scatter means to spread out.

The fruits of a maple tree
look like wings. This shape
helps them scatter.

The fruits of a
water lily have
seeds. The fruits
float on water.

Fruits cover seeds.
Fruits keep seeds safe.
Fruits help scatter seeds.
Some fruits travel by air or water.
Some fruits get stuck on animals.
Animals carry seeds to new places.

Burrs are fruits. They hook onto animals. This dog will help scatter the seeds in these burrs.

How are plants grouped?

One group of plants has flowers.
The other group of plants does not
have flowers.

Plants with flowers grow in many places.
They can grow in gardens, fields, or deserts.

A cactus grows in the desert.
It has flowers that make seeds.
New cactus plants grow from
the seeds.

Trees are plants.
Some trees have flowers.
Peach trees grow flowers.
The flowers make peaches.
Peaches are fruits.
Fruits cover peach seeds and keep them safe.

Plants without Flowers

Some plants do not have flowers.
Some plants have cones.
The seeds grow inside the cones.
The cone opens and seeds fall out.
The seeds grow into new trees.

**Pine trees have
cones with seeds.**

Ferns do not have flowers.
Ferns do not make seeds.
Ferns have leaves, roots, and stems.

Ferns live in warm,
shady, wet places.

How are some woodland plants adapted?

Living things have **adapted,** or changed, to live in many places.
An **environment** is a place with living and nonliving things.

A woodland is a kind of environment.
Pine trees are adapted to the cold.

Maple trees are adapted to warm summers and cold winters.
Maple trees have big, flat leaves.
These leaves drop off in the fall.
This helps the tree store water for the winter.

Plants that Live Near Water

Some plants in a woodland environment live near water.
These plants are adapted to live where it is wet.

This red plant is called a cardinal plant. Its roots are adapted to get nutrients from wet soil.

Cardinal plant

The stinging nettle has sharp hairs to help keep it safe from animals that want to eat it.

The fanwort is adapted to live in water.

How are some prairie plants adapted?

Many plants live in a prairie environment. A **prairie** has lots of grass and few trees.

Many prairies have hot summers with little rain.
Some prairie plants are adapted to hold water.
This helps when it does not rain.

Goldenrod plants have stiff stems and leaves. This helps the plants keep the water they need to live.

Prairie smoke has fuzz that traps air. The air helps the plant hold water.

Prairie grasses have small leaves that help hold water.

How are some desert plants adapted?

Many deserts are sunny and hot all day.
Deserts can be cool at night.
Deserts get little rain.

Some desert plants are adapted to hold water for a long time.

Some leaves on a desert almond stay out of the sun. These leaves can hold water in the plant.

The saguaro cactus has a long, thick stem. The stem holds water.

The octopus tree has short leaves and long spines. The spines keep the plant safe from animals that want to eat it.

How are some marsh plants adapted?

A marsh is a wet environment. Many plants grow in a marsh.

The soil in a marsh may not have many nutrients. Plants in a marsh get nutrients in other ways.

Cattails grow in wet soil. They are adapted to get nutrients from water in the soil.

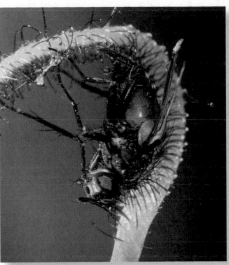

A sundew plant has hairs that trap insects. The plant gets some nutrients from the insects.

A venus's flytrap also gets some nutrients from insects.

Plants are adapted to their environments.
Plants live in many kinds of places.

Every plant needs food, water, air, and sunlight to grow!

Glossary

adapted   changed to be able to live in a certain environment

environment   a kind of place with living and nonliving things

flower   the part of a plant that makes seeds or fruit

leaves   flat, green parts growing from the stem of a plant

nutrients   food that living things need to grow

prairie   a place with flat land, a lot of grass, and a few trees

roots   parts of a plant that grows into the ground

stem   the part of a plant that grows up from the ground